Homemade Bread:

30 Easy Recipes For Excellent Baking At Home

Disclaimer: All photos used in this book, including the cover photo were made available under a Attribution-Non Commercial-Share Alike 2.0 Generic and sourced from Flickr

Table of content:

Introduction 5
Chapter 1: Why make your bread? 6
Chapter 2: Classic Delicious Bread Recipes 15
    1. Buttermilk Bread 15
    2. Classic Sandwich Loaf 17
    3. Banana Bread 19
    4. Homemade Foccacia 22
    5. Apple Walnut Loaf 24
    6. Yogurt & Bran Bread 26
    7. Homemade Buttermilk Cornbread 28
    8. Melted Muenster Bun 30
    9. Blue Ribbon Bread 32
Chapter 3: Delicious Bread Recipes 34
    10. All That Jazz 34
    11. Bread and Butter 36
    12. Back to Basics Bread 38
    13. Inside Outside Bread 40
    14. Picnic Bread 42
    15. Sandwich Bread 44
    16. Fairy Bread 46
    17. Anadama Bread 48
    18. Farmhouse Loaf 50
    19. Granary Bread 52
Chapter 4: Mouth Mumbling Bread Recipes 54
    20. Light Whole Meal Bread 54
    21. Basic White Bread 56
    22. Milk Loaf 58

23.	Fig & Hazelnut Bread	60
24.	Three Cheese Bread	62
25.	Russian Black Bread	64
26.	Rice Bread	66
27.	Potato Bread	68
28.	Malted Loaf	70
29.	Light Rye and Caraway Bread	72
30.	Grainy Beer & Mustard Loaf	74

Conclusion **76**

Introduction

Bread has been a staple food of humans for ages, and has developed from more primitive flatbreads – some even cooked in hot coals – to more complex bread that use yeast and sugar to gain their texture and taste. Since we use bread so much, why keep buying the same old boring, processed bread from the grocery store when you can easily make it fresh? Baking your bread is not only rewarding, but allows you to control what goes into your bread and by extension your body.

This recipe book aims to include all kinds of bread – from the kind you can use every day in your kitchen, to rolls and biscuits, to sweet and fruity bread that is great for dessert or brunch. With such a variety of homemade bread to try, you'll always have something tasty waiting in your kitchen and something aromatic in the oven!

Chapter 1: Why make your bread?

The savings of making your bread are immense; it's rare for a homemade loaf of bread to cost more than a dollar. Compare that to the prices you find on the shelf in the grocery store and consider the fact that you'll probably go through several loaves of bread each week.

Of course, that store-bought loaf doesn't just come with a higher price tag; it also comes with dough conditioners, additives, preservatives, and a heap of sugar. That loaf is jam-packed with tasty sounding things like calcium propionate, calcium sulphate, and potassium iodate.

All that extra money you're spending isn't just buying you convenience; it's also buying you a handful of strange chemicals you need to look upon the Internet to understand. I would argue that learning how to bloom yeast, knead the dough, and bake a tasty loaf at home is much less complicated than figuring out what kind of strange chemicals you're feeding your family every day, wouldn't you?

Understanding flour

Wheat flours

Different types of wheat make different types of flour. Not every kind of flour can make quality bread dough. Protein content is the most influential factor in determining if a type of flour should be used for bread. The protein content of most flours is directly related to the available gluten that flour can create.

Gluten is a large protein molecule that, when hydrated, forms protein chains that tangle together and give the dough the structure that holds it together. This structure then captures the gas bubbles created by yeast, steam, or chemical leavening agents that cause the bread to rise.

Cake flour

Cake flour has a very low protein content, averaging around 7 to 9 percent. As a result, it has a very low amount of available gluten. While this makes for soft, tender cakes, and pastries, it has little of the structure required for making bread. Cake flour is also treated with chlorine dioxide or chlorine gas to help whiten it. This chemical change makes cake flour more acidic and less hospitable for yeast.

Whole wheat flour

Whole wheat flour has high protein content, averaging between 11 and 15 percent. Unfortunately, not all of this protein is available as gluten. A large amount of the protein in whole wheat flour is locked up in the germ and bran coating that is ground into the flour. While wheat germ and bran contribute healthy nutrients as well as fibre, they ultimately interfere with gluten formation.

Bread dough made completely from whole wheat flour will not have enough gluten to maintain a significant rise. As a result, unless you like very dense, heavy bread, it can be a good idea to add a little all-purpose or bread flour to whole wheat bread.

All-purpose flour

All-purpose flour has modest protein content averaging between 11 and 12 percent. This amount of available gluten works well with bread that uses chemical leavening agents. While all-purpose flour can be used to make a yeast-leavened bread, it doesn't usually have the same rise as dough made from bread flour.

It is also worth noting that because all-purpose flour comes from regional blends of ground wheat, the protein content can be inconsistent from one bag of flour to the next.

Bread flour

Bread flour averages between 12 and 13 percent protein content. As a result, it has enough available gluten to make a dough that will be sturdy enough to trap the gasses released by yeast.

Self-rising flour

Self-rising flour is a blend of all-purpose flour combined with the chemical leavening agent baking powder. It is often used for quick bread and pastries. However, it should not be used for yeast-raised bread dough. Self-rising flour often requires sifting, or whisking, to break up any small clumps before being incorporated into the wet ingredients. Self-rising flour should be stored in a sealed container, and kept in low humidity to prolong the shelf-life of the baking powder.

Gluten-free flours

People who experience celiac disease, or who are otherwise intolerant to wheat flours and gluten, need alternative flours to produce bread. Luckily for these people, the marketplace is awash with alternative flour blends.

These gluten-free flours are blends of different flours and starches which are then supplemented with xanthan gum. This naturally occurring gum is an emulsifier that can behave like gluten. These specialty blends are all specific to the manufacturer, so you need to read the label closely.

A quick rule of thumb for determining if a gluten-free flour blend can be used for making bread is to look at the grams of protein per quarter cup. All-purpose flour averages 3 grams of protein per quarter. A gluten-free flour blend that has 3 grams of protein per quarter cup should be able to replicate the role of all-purpose flour.

For easy source, here is a list of flours and starches that are gluten-free:

- Rice flour (including brown rice flour and rice starch)
- Potato starch
- Corn flour, cornmeal and cornstarch
- Tapioca flour and starch (tapioca is sometimes also called cassava or manioc)
- Amaranth flour
- Arrowroot
- Millet flour
- Quinoa flour
- Sorghum flour
- Lupin flour
- Buckwheat flour (despite the name, buckwheat has no relation to wheat)
- Almond meal (and other nut flours)
- Coconut flour
- Garbanzo, fava, soy, and other legume flours
- Meals made from chia seeds, flaxseeds, and other seeds

As you can see, there are plenty of options for people needing to avoid gluten!

Chapter 2: Classic Delicious Bread Recipes

1. Buttermilk Bread

Servings: 2-4

Preparation Time: 60 to 80 minutes

Ingredients:

- 1 1/2 teaspoons of easy-blend dried yeast
- 1 ½ teaspoons of salt
- 1 ½ cups of wholemeal brand flour
- 3 cups of white bread flour
- 1 ½ tablespoons of sunflower oil
- 1 ½ tablespoons of clear organic honey
- 4 ½ tablespoons of water
- 1 ½ cups of buttermilk

Directions:

1. Place the water, honey, sunflower oil, buttermilk, inside of the bread machine tin.

2. Scatter the white flour and the wholemeal flour together all over the liquid mixture.

3. Put salt on the edge of the tin.

4. Place a small hole in the middle of the mixture and place the yeast inside it.

5. Set the machine to the basic-normal setting, medium crust and begin the process.

6. When finished, remove your bread from the tin.

7. Place the bread on a wire rack and allow it to cool down.

2. Classic Sandwich Loaf

Prep time: 60 minutes

Servings: 6

Ingredients:

- 2 cups whole wheat flour
- 4 1/2 cups warm water
- 1 1/2 tablespoons salt
- 2/3 cup brown sugar
- 2/3 cup vegetable oil
- 10 cups bread flour
- 1/2 cup warm water
- 3 packs (25oz) active dry yeast
- 1/4 cup bread flour
- 1 tablespoon white sugar
- 2 cups quick cooking oats

Directions:

1. Combine 1/2 cup warm water, 1 tablespoon sugar, 1/4 cup bread flour and yeast. Let it sit for around 5 minutes.

2. Add oats, 4 1/2 water, whole wheat flour, 2/3 cup sugar, 2/3 cup of oil and salt. Mix using an electric mixer running at low speed for about 2 minutes.

3. Gradually add bread flour, half a cup at a time until dough pulls away from the bowl.

4. Grease another bowl and transfer mixture. Wrap with a damp cloth and let it sit for an hour until it rises.

5. Once ready, place mixture in a greased loaf pan. Allow rising again for another hour.

6. Place in an oven for half an hour at 350 degrees.

7. Allow cooling before serving.

3. Banana Bread

Banana bread is one of the most delicious and nutritious bread that you can prepare at home. You can buy it from a store, but the ones sold on the market contain a lot of dairy products, eggs and preservatives. For this reason, they are higher in calorie and cholesterol. In this passage, we will be preparing fresh banana bread without adding any dairy products. This will allow the bread to last longer and taste better. If you prefer eggs, then you can add them.

Ingredients

- Flour – 2 cups
- Unrefined sugar – 3/4 cup
- Brown sugar – 1/2 cup
- Baking soda – 3/4 tbsp
- Cinnamon – 3/4 tbsp
- Almond milk or soy milk – 1/2 cup

- Apple vinegar – 1 tbsp
- Mashed bananas – 2 cups
- Canola oil – 1/4 cup
- Agave syrup or maple syrup – 2 tbsp
- Vanilla extract – 1 tbsp

Directions

1. For preparing banana bread, you need to preheat your oven to a temperature of around 180 C. Next you need a medium-sized loaf dish. If your dish is small, then you may use 2 of them. You should apply some olive margarine on your loaf dish and keep it prepared for baking. Next, you can begin to prepare your dough.

2. Take the flour in a big bowl and add baking soda, cinnamon and sugar into it. Mix all the ingredients with your hand.

3. Take another bowl and mix apple vinegar and milk. This mixture would take around 2 minutes to blend. To this mixture, you may add the mashed banana, vanilla extract and canola oil. With the help of a whisk blend the ingredients until everything combines with each other.

4. Now you can add this mixture to the first bowl that contains the flour mixture. Mix everything into a soft mixture. Next, you should pour the mixture into your loaf dish and keep it in the oven. Bake for an entire hour until the dough or the mixture becomes firm and soft. You can test the bread after one hour by inserting a toothpick. If the toothpick comes out pretty clean, then your bread is ready. Otherwise, you would need to bake it for another 10 to 15 minutes. Once you are done, remove the bread and keep it aside until it is cool enough to be served. This banana bread is delicious, and you can serve it as a special breakfast with tea or coffee.

5. This is simple banana bread which is prepared without adding an egg or any dairy products. You can make this bread more delicious and rich by adding some dried fruits like raisins, cashew nuts, walnuts and almonds. You can even add chocolate chips if you like the chocolate flavor. Some people do not prefer eggless preparations. If you are one among them, then you can add an egg or two and make the bread more delicious. In the same way, you can reduce the amount of sugar if you do not like much sugar in your food or if you are on dieting.

6. If your oven takes time to heat, then it would be better to cook the bread in two different trays. By dividing the dough, you can reduce the burden on your oven.

4. Homemade Foccacia

Prep time: 90 minutes
Servings: the 4-6

Ingredients:

- 3 1/2 cups all-purpose flour
- 1 teaspoon white sugar
- 1 teaspoon salt
- 1 tablespoon active dry yeast
- 1 cup water
- 2 tablespoons vegetable oil
- 1 egg
- 3 tablespoons olive oil
- 1 teaspoon dried rosemary, crushed

Directions:

1. Mix flour, yeast, salt and sugar.

2. Heat water and vegetable oil—add both to the mixture.

3. Crack the egg into the bowl and blend all ingredients with an electric mixer.

4. Add 1 3/4 cup of flour.

5. Knead the dough and let it sit for about 5 minutes and shape into a loaf.

6. Wrap with a towel and let it sit for about half an hour.

7. Once ready, take a fork and poke through the tops.

8. Drizzle with olive oil and top with rosemary.

9. Bake for 15-25 minutes at 400 degrees.

5. Apple Walnut Loaf

Prep time: 120 minutes
Servings: 4-6

Ingredients:

- 3 cups all-purpose flour
- 1 teaspoon baking soda
- 1 teaspoon salt
- 1 cup chopped walnuts
- 3 cups apples - peeled, cored, and cut
- 1 cup vegetable oil
- 2 cups white sugar
- 3 eggs, beaten
- 2 teaspoons ground cinnamon

Directions:

1. Set oven to 300 degrees.

2. Combine baking soda with flour, salt, walnuts and apples.

3. In another bowl, combine sugar, oil, cinnamon and eggs.

4. Combine both and mix.

5. Divide batter into two, greased loaf pans and place in the oven.

6. Bake for 90 minutes.

6. Yogurt & Bran Bread

Servings: 2-4
Preparation time: 60-80 minutes

Ingredients:

- 1 teaspoon of dried yeast
- 1 ½ teaspoons of salt
- ½ cup of wheat bran
- 1 2/3 cups whole-meal bread flour
- 2 ½ cups of white bread flour
- 2 tablespoons of molasses
- 1 ½ tablespoons of sunflower oil
- ½ cup of natural yoghurt
- ¾ cup of water

Directions:

1. Place the molasses, water, sunflower oil and yoghurt into the bread machine tin.

2. Scatter the white and whole-meal flour together over the mix in the tin.

3. Add salt and wheat bran inside as well.

4. Make a small hole in the middle of the flour and place the yeast in the hole.

5. Set the machine to the basic-normal setting, medium crust and begin the baking process.

6. When the bread is done, remove it from the tin, placing it on a wire rack to cool.

7. Homemade Buttermilk Cornbread

Prep time: 60 minutes
Servings: 8

Ingredients:

- 1/2 cup butter
- 2/3 cup white sugar
- 2 eggs
- 1 cup buttermilk
- 1/2 teaspoon baking soda
- 1 cup cornmeal
- 1 cup all-purpose flour
- 1/2 teaspoon salt

Directions:

1. Set oven to 375 degrees.

2. Melt sugar over low heat and add sugar.

3. Add eggs and beat into the mixture until well blended.

4. Add baking soda and buttermilk; mix in cornmeal, flour and salt. Once smooth, pour into a square baking pan.

5. Bake for 30-40 minutes.

8. Melted Muenster Bun

Prep time: 80 minutes
Servings: 6

Ingredients:

- 3 1/2 teaspoons white sugar
- 2 teaspoons salt
- 1 tablespoon active dry yeast
- 4 cups all-purpose flour
- 1/2 cup margarine
- 1 cup milk
- 1 egg
- 1 egg yolk
- 2 pounds Muenster cheese, shredded
- 1 egg white, beaten
- 2 tablespoons whole blanched almonds

Directions:

1. Combine butter and milk in a skillet over low heat.

2. IN a bowl, combine yeast, sugar and salt. Add milk mixture. Beat mixture for about 2 minutes.

3. Regularly add 1 cup of flour while beating until you achieve a soft dough.

4. Place dough on a floured surface and knead until smooth. Cover and provide to rest for 15 minutes.

5. Combine egg and egg yolk with shredded cheese.

6. Once the dough is ready, take a rolling pin and roll dough flat.

7. Place cheese mixture in the middle and fold dough around it. Pinch seams to seal and cover with a towel while you let it rest for about 10 minutes.

8. Once ready, brush with egg white and sprinkle with blanched almonds.

9. Bake for an hour at 350 degrees.

9. Blue Ribbon Bread

Ingredients:

- 1 ¼ cup water
- 1 ½ teaspoons salt
- 1 ½ tablespoons vegan butter
- 2 tablespoons stevia
- 1 ½ tablespoons dried milk
- 3 ¾ cups flour
- 1 ½ teaspoons active yeast

Directions:

1. You can use either a kitchen mixer, a bread machine or something similar, or you can mix the bread by hand. You are going to start with adding all the dry ingredients to a bowl and mixing them thoroughly.

2. Next, add in the wet ingredients one at a time. Make sure each one is thoroughly blended before adding the next and make sure there are no lumps. Leave it to rise for one hour. Either use your hand or the bread machine to mix the dough once more, then let it rise once again.

3. Divide the dough into loaves and shape into the proper size, then place in bread pans.

4. Preheat oven to 350 degrees F while the dough rises a second time.

5. Place the loaves in the oven and bake for 40 to 45 minutes.

6. Remove from oven and let stand for a few minutes before removing from the pans, then turn out on the counter and let cool.

Chapter 3: Delicious Bread Recipes

10. All That Jazz

Ingredients:

- 1 ¼ cup water
- 1 ½ teaspoons salt
- 1 ½ tablespoons coconut oil
- 2 tablespoons sugar
- 1 ½ tablespoons dried milk
- 3 ¾ cups coconut flour
- 1 ½ teaspoons active yeast

Directions:

1. You can use either a bread machine, a kitchen mixer or something similar, or you can mix the bread by hand. You are going to start with adding all the dry ingredients to a bowl and mixing them thoroughly.

2. Next, add in the wet ingredients one at a time. Make sure each one is thoroughly blended before adding the next and make sure there are no lumps. Leave it to rise for one hour. Either use your hand or the bread machine to mix the dough once more, then let it rise once again.

3. Divide the dough into loaves and shape into the proper size, then place in bread pans.

4. Preheat oven to 350 degrees F while the dough rises a second time.

5. Place the loaves in the oven and bake for 40 to 45 minutes.

6. Remove from oven and let stand for a few minutes before removing from the pans, then turn out on the counter and let cool.

11. Bread and Butter

Ingredients:

- 1 ¼ cup water
- 1 ½ teaspoons salt
- 1 tablespoon butter
- 2 tablespoons stevia
- 1 tablespoon vegetable oil
- 1 ½ tablespoons dried milk
- 3 ¾ cups flour
- 1 ½ teaspoons active yeast

Directions:

1. You can use either a bread machine, a kitchen mixer or something similar, or you can mix the bread by hand. You are going to start with adding all the dry ingredients to a bowl and mixing them thoroughly.

2. Next, add in the wet ingredients one at a time. Make sure each one is thoroughly blended before adding the next and make sure there are no lumps. Leave it to rise for one hour. Either use your hand or the bread machine to mix the dough once more, then let it rise once again.

3. Divide the dough into loaves and shape into the proper size, then place in bread pans.

4. Preheat oven to 350 degrees F while the dough rises a second time.

5. Place the loaves in the oven and bake for 40 to 45 minutes.

6. Remove from oven and let stand for a few minutes before removing from the pans, then turn out on the counter and let cool.

12. Back to Basics Bread

Ingredients:

- 1 ¼ cup water
- 1 teaspoon salt
- 1 ½ tablespoons vegetable oil
- 2 tablespoons sugar
- 1 ½ tablespoons dried milk
- 3 ¾ cups potato flour
- 1 ½ teaspoons active yeast

Directions:

1. You can use either a bread machine, a kitchen mixer or something similar, or you can mix the bread by hand. You are going to start with adding all the dry ingredients to a bowl and mixing them thoroughly.

2. Next, add in the wet ingredients one at a time. Make sure each one is thoroughly blended before adding the next and make sure there are no lumps. Leave it to rise for one hour. Either use your hand or the bread machine to mix the dough once more, then let it rise once again.

3. Divide the dough into loaves and shape into the proper size, then place in bread pans.

4. Preheat oven to 350 degrees F while the dough rises a second time.

5. Place the loaves in the oven and bake for 40 to 45 minutes.

6. Remove from oven and let stand for a few minutes before removing from the pans, then turn out on the counter and let cool.

13. Inside Outside Bread

Ingredients:

- 1 ¼ cup milk
- 1 ½ teaspoons salt
- 1 ½ tablespoons butter
- 2 tablespoons honey
- 1 ½ tablespoons dried milk
- 3 ¾ cups whole wheat flour
- 1 ½ teaspoons active yeast

Directions:

1. You can use either a bread machine, a kitchen mixer or something similar, or you can mix the bread by hand. You are going to start with adding all the dry ingredients to a bowl and mixing them thoroughly.

2. Next, add in the wet ingredients one at a time. Make sure each one is thoroughly blended before adding the next and make sure there are no lumps. Leave it to rise for one hour. Either use your hand or the bread machine to mix the dough once more, then let it rise once again.

3. Divide the dough into loaves and shape into the proper size, then place in bread pans.

4. Preheat oven to 350 degrees F while the dough rises a second time.

5. Place the loaves in the oven and bake for 40 to 45 minutes.

6. Remove from oven and let stand for a few minutes before removing from the pans, then turn out on the counter and let cool.

14. Picnic Bread

Ingredients:

- 1 ¼ cup almond milk
- 1 ½ teaspoons salt
- 1 ½ tablespoons butter
- 2 tablespoons sugar
- 1 ½ tablespoons dried milk
- 3 ¾ cups almond flour
- 1 ½ teaspoons active yeast

Directions:

1. You can use either a bread machine, a kitchen mixer or something similar, or you can mix the bread by hand. You are going to start with adding all the dry ingredients to a bowl and mixing them thoroughly.

2. Next, add in the wet ingredients one at a time. Make sure each one is thoroughly blended before adding the next and make sure there are no lumps. Leave it to rise for one hour. Either use your hand or the bread machine to mix the dough once more, then let it rise once again.

3. Divide the dough into loaves and shape into the proper size, then place in bread pans.

4. Preheat oven to 350 degrees F while the dough rises a second time.

5. Place the loaves in the oven and bake for 40 to 45 minutes.

6. Remove from oven and let stand for a few minutes before removing from the pans, then turn out on the counter and let cool.

15. Sandwich Bread

Ingredients:

- 1 ¼ cup water
- 1 ½ teaspoons salt
- 1 ½ tablespoons olive oil
- 2 tablespoons sugar
- 1 ½ tablespoons dried milk
- 3 ¾ cups almond flour
- 1 tablespoon cinnamon
- 1 ½ teaspoons active yeast

Directions:

1. You can use either a bread machine, a kitchen mixer or something similar, or you can mix the bread by hand. You are going to start with adding all the dry ingredients to a bowl and mixing them thoroughly.

2. Next, add in the wet ingredients one at a time. Make sure each one is thoroughly blended before adding the next and make sure there are no lumps. Leave it to rise for one hour. Either use your hand or the bread machine to mix the dough once more, then let it rise once again.

3. Divide the dough into loaves and shape into the proper size, then place in bread pans.

4. Preheat oven to 350 degrees F while the dough rises a second time.

5. Place the loaves in the oven and bake for 40 to 45 minutes. The loaves are done when they are golden brown.

6. Remove from oven and let stand for a few minutes before removing from the pans, then turn out on the counter and let cool.

16. Fairy Bread

Ingredients:

- 1 ¼ cup coconut milk
- 1 ½ teaspoons salt
- 1 ½ tablespoons coconut oil
- 2 tablespoons sugar
- 1 ½ tablespoons dried milk
- 3 ¾ cups coconut flour
- 1 ½ teaspoons active yeast

Directions:

1. You can use either a bread machine, a kitchen mixer or something similar, or you can mix the bread by hand. You are going to start with adding all the dry ingredients to a bowl and mixing them thoroughly.

2. Next, add in the wet ingredients one at a time. Make sure each one is thoroughly blended before adding the next and make sure there are no lumps. Leave it to rise for one hour. Either use your hand or the bread machine to mix the dough once more, then let it rise once again.

3. Divide the dough into loaves and shape into the proper size, then place in bread pans.

4. Preheat oven to 350 degrees F while the dough rises a second time.

5. Place the loaves in the oven and bake for 40 to 45 minutes.

6. Remove from oven and let stand for a few minutes before removing from the pans, then turn out on the counter and let cool.

17. Anadama Bread

This type of bread is a traditional New England bread that is made with a mixture of white and wholemeal flours and polenta, which is a coarse corn-meal. The molasses sweetens the bread and gives it a nice rich colour.

Servings: 2-4
Preparation time: 60-80 minutes

Ingredients:

- 3 cups of white bread flour
- 1 teaspoon of lemon juice
- 4 tablespoons of molasses
- 1 cup of water
- 1 teaspoon of dried yeast
- 3 tablespoons of butter
- 2 teaspoons of salt
- ½ cup of polenta
- ¾ cup of whole-meal bread flour

Directions:

1. Place the molasses, water and lemon juice into the bread machine tin.

2. Scatter in the white flour and the whole-meal flour over the liquid mixture.

3. Scatter the polenta over the mixture.

4. Place salt and butter in different places in the tin.

5. Make a small hole in the middle of the tin and add the yeast into the hole.

6. Place the machine on the basic-normal setting, medium crust and begin the process.

7. When the bread is done, remove it from the tin and place it on a wire rack to cool.

18. Farmhouse Loaf

Servings: 2-4
Preparation time: 60-80 minutes

Ingredients:

- 1 ½ cups of skimmed milk powder
- 1 teaspoon of dried yeast
- 2 tablespoons of butter
- 1 ½ teaspoons of granulated sugar
- 1 ½ teaspoons of salt
- ½ cup of whole-meal bread flour
- 3 ½ cups of white bread flour
- 1 ½ cups of water

Directions:

1. Put water into the bread machine tin.

2. Scatter the whole-meal and white flour over the water.

3. Add sugar and salt, along with butter in different places inside the tin.

4. Make a small hole in the middle of the mixture, then place yeast into the hole.

5. Set the machine to the basic-normal setting, medium crust and begin the bread making process.

6. Ten minutes before the bread baking time is completed, brush the top of loaf with some water.

7. Dust a little white bread flour as well on the top.

8. With a knife cut the top of the bread.

9. When it is finished, remove bread from tin and place it on a wire rack to cool.

19. Granary Bread

Granary flour is very like malt-house flour; it is a blend that contains malted wheat grain, which gives a crunchy texture to the loaf. You would also sprinkle some wheat grain on top of the loaf before the baking started.

Serving: 2-4
Preparation time: 60-80

Ingredients:

- 1 ½ teaspoons of salt
- 4 ½ cups of granary bread flour
- 1 ½ cups of water
- 1 ½ teaspoons of dried yeast
- 2 tablespoons of butter
- 1 tablespoon of granulated sugar

Directions:

1. Place the water in the bread machine tin.

2. Scatter the flour on top of the water.

3. Add in sugar, salt and butter, in different areas of the tin.

4. Make a small hole in the middle of the mixture and place the yeast into the hole.

5. Set the bread machine on the whole wheat or multi-grain setting, medium crust and proceed.

6. When the bread is done, remove it from the tin and place it onto a wire rack to cool.

Chapter 4: Mouth Mumbling Bread Recipes

20. Light Whole Meal Bread

This type of bread is very tasty, and light. It becomes a light loaf just by adding some white flour. Another option is to replace the whole-meal flour with brown flour.

Servings: 2-4
Preparation time: 60-80

Ingredients:

- 3 cups of wholemeal bread flour
- 1 ½ cups of water
- 1 ½ teaspoons of easy-blend dried yeast
- 2 tablespoons of butter
- 2 teaspoons of granulated sugar
- 2 teaspoons of salt
- 1 ½ cups white bread flour

Directions:

1. Place water into the bread machine tin.

2. Scatter the white and whole-meal flour over the water.

3. Add in butter, salt and sugar in different areas in the tin.

4. Make a small hole in the center of the mixture and add the yeast to the hole.

5. Set the bread machine to the basic-normal setting, medium crust and start the bread making process.

6. When the bread is done, remove it from tin and place it on a wire rack to cool.

21. Basic White Bread

A basic white loaf can be cooked on the fastest setting that is ideal if you are in a hurry. On the quick setting, the yeast has less time to work so your bread may not rise as high.

Servings: 2-4
Preparation time: 60-80

Ingredients:

- 2 tablespoons of sunflower oil
- 1 ½ cups of water
- 1 ½ teaspoons of easy-blend dried yeast
- 1 ½ teaspoons of granulated sugar
- 1 ½ teaspoons of salt
- 1 ½ tablespoons of skimmed milk powder
- 4 ½ cups unbleached white bread flour

Directions:

1. Add the sunflower oil and water into the bread machine tin.

2. Scatter the flour on top of the liquid.

3. Add the milk powder, sugar, and salt in different areas in the tin.

4. Make a small hole in the middle of the mixture, add yeast into the hole.

5. Set the machine to the rapid-quick setting, medium crust and start the bread making process.

6. When the bread is done, remove it from tin and place it on a wire rack to cool.

22. Milk Loaf

When you add milk to your bread, the result is soft bread. Milk is also good for helping to preserve the quality of the bread. The milk should be room temperature or it will retard the action of the yeast and the bread will not rise properly.

Servings: 2-4
Preparation time: 60-80 minutes

Ingredients:

- 4 cups of unbleached white bread flour
- 7 tablespoons of water
- ¾ cup of milk
- 1 teaspoon of dried yeast
- 2 tablespoons of butter
- 2 teaspoons of granulated sugar
- 1 ½ teaspoons of salt

Directions:

1. Place the milk and water into the bread machine tin.

2. Scatter the flour on top of the liquid.

3. Add sugar, salt and butter in different areas within the tin.

4. Make a small hole in the middle of the mixture, adding the yeast into the hole.

5. Set the bread machine to the basic-normal setting, medium crust, and begin the bread making process.

6. When the bread is done, remove it from the tin and place it on a wire rack to cool.

23. Fig & Hazelnut Bread

This bread gives you a very delicious flavour, and it is perfect for breakfast. You can replace the figs with other dried fruits.

Servings: 4-6
Preparation time: 60-80 minutes

Ingredients:

- 1 ½ teaspoons of lemon juice
- ½ a cup of hazelnuts, toasted, chopped
- ¼ cup of dried figs, coarsely chopped
- 1 ½ teaspoons of dried yeast
- 2 tablespoons of butter
- 1 tablespoon of sugar
- 1 ½ teaspoons of salt
- 2 tablespoons of skimmed milk powder
- 4 tablespoons of toasted wheat germ
- 1 cup of brown flour
- 3 cups of white flour

Directions:

1. Place the lemon juice, and water in the bread machine tin.

2. Scatter the wheat germ and flours all over the top of the liquid.

3. Scatter the milk powder on top as well.

4. Place sugar, salt and butter in different areas of the tin.

5. Create a small hole in the centre of the mixture, add the yeast to the hole.

6. Set the machine to the basic-normal setting, medium crust and begin the bread making process.

7. Put the hazelnuts and figs as soon as the machine beeps.

8. When the bread is finished, remove it from tin, place it on a wire rack to cool.

24. Three Cheese Bread

Using a wonderful trio of Italian cheeses will give you a great flavour of this three-cheese bread. You can also replace the cheeses with other cheeses such as cheddar for example. This bread goes great with soup or a salad.

Servings: 2-4
Preparation time: 60-80 minutes

Ingredients:

- 1 tablespoon of wheat flakes
- 3 tablespoons of chives, fresh, chopped
- 1 cup of parmesan cheese, grated
- 3 tablespoons of gorgonzola cheese, diced
- 1 ½ teaspoons of dried yeast
- 1 teaspoon of salt
- 2 teaspoons of granulated sugar
- ½ cup of granary flour
- 3 ½ cups of white bread flour
- 5 tablespoons of mascarpone cheese
- 1 egg yolk
- 1 egg
- ¾ cup of water

Directions:

1. Put the water, mascarpone cheese and egg into the bread machine tin.
2. Scatter the white flour and the granary flour over the cheese mixture.
3. Put salt and sugar in different places in the tin.
4. Create a small hole in the middle of the mixture and add into it the yeast.
5. Place the bread machine on dough setting, medium crust and begin the bread making process.
6. Set aside the gorgonzola, parmesan and chives, add them when the machine begins to beep.
7. When the dough cycle is finished, transfer the dough to the floured surface.
8. Punch down the dough gently and shape it into a round loaf.
9. Cover it with oiled clear film and leave it to rest in a warm place for about 45 minutes.
10. Preheat oven to 400F.
11. Mix the egg yolk with one tablespoon of water and brush over the top of dough.
12. Scatter the wheat flakes and bake for 35 minutes or until golden.
13. When the cooking is done, remove the bread from the pan of the machine.
14. Place the bread on a wire rack to cool.

25. Russian Black Bread

European rye bread often include cocoa and coffee in their recipes to add colour to this dark traditionally dense and chewy bread. Slice it thin and serve with cold meats or pates or use it to make an open sandwich.

Servings: 2-4
Preparation time: 60-80 minutes

Ingredients:

- 2 ½ tablespoons of molasses
- 1 ½ teaspoons of dried yeast
- 1 ½ teaspoon of salt
- 1 ½ teaspoons of caraway seeds
- 2 ½ tablespoons of instant coffee granules
- 1 ½ tablespoons of cocoa powder
- ¾ cup of dried breadcrumbs
- 3 tablespoons of oat bran
- 2 ¼ cups of white bread flour
- ¾ cup of whole-meal bread flour

- 1 ¼ cups of rye flour
- 2 tablespoons of sunflower oil
- 1 ½ cups of water

Directions:

1. Place the molasses, water and sunflower oil into the bread machine tin.

2. Scatter the white flour, the rye flour, and whole-meal flour all together in the tin.

3. Scatter the cocoa powder, coffee granules, salt and caraway seeds.

4. Create a small hole in the middle of the mixture and place yeast in the hole.

5. Put the machine on whole wheat setting, medium crust, and begin the bread making process.

6. When the bread is done, remove the bread and place it on a wire rack to cool.

26. Rice Bread

Rice is an unusual ingredient, but it does make delicious bread that is moist and has a nice texture.

Servings: 2-4
Preparation time: 60-80 minutes

Ingredients:

- 1 ¼ cups of cooked long grain rice, well drained
- 1 teaspoon of dried yeast
- 1 tablespoon of butter
- 2 tablespoons of granulated sugar
- 1 ½ teaspoons of salt
- 1 ½ tablespoons of skimmed milk powder
- 3 ¾ cups of white bread flour
- 1 cup of water

Directions:

1. Put the water into the bread machine tin.

2. Put in the egg, no need for it to be beaten.

3. Scatter the flour all over the water-egg mixture.

4. Scatter the rice and milk powder too.

5. Place sugar, salt and butter in different areas within the tin.

6. Create a small hole in the middle of the mixture and place the yeast inside the hole.

7. Place the machine on the basic-normal setting, medium crust and begin the bread making process.

8. When your bread is done, remove it from tin and place it on a wire rack to cool.

27. Potato Bread

This is a nice moist and soft golden crusty loaf; it is perfect for making sandwiches with. Try and use the water that you cooked the potatoes in to make your bread.

Servings: 2-4
Preparation time: 60-80 minutes

Ingredients:

- 1 tablespoon of sunflower oil
- 1 ½ teaspoons of dried yeast
- 2 teaspoons of granulated sugar
- 1 ½ teaspoons of salt
- 1 ½ tablespoons of skimmed milk powder
- 2 cups of mashed potato, cold
- 4 ½ cups of white flour bread

Directions:

1. Add the sunflower oil and water into the bread machine tin.

2. Scatter the flour all over the water mix.

3. Scatter the mashed potato and the milk powder too.

4. Add salt and sugar in different areas of the tin.

5. Create a small hole in the middle of the mix and add the yeast.

6. Set the machine to the basic-normal setting, medium crust and begin the bread making process.

7. When your bread is done, remove it from the tin and place it on a wire rack to cool.

28. Malted Loaf

A malt and sultana loaf makes a great breakfast or tea time bread. Serve sliced and spread with butter. You could glaze the loaf in the end by dissolving one tablespoon of caster sugar and one tablespoon of milk and brush this over the crust.

Servings: 2-4
Preparation time: 60-80 minutes

Ingredients:

- 2 tablespoons of malt extract
- 1 ½ tablespoons of golden syrup
- 1 ¼ cups of water
- ½ cup of sultanas
- 1 teaspoon of dried yeast
- ¼ cup of butter
- 1 teaspoon of salt
- 2 tablespoons of skimmed milk powder
- 4 ½ cups of white bread flour

Directions:

1. Place the malt extract, golden syrup and water into the bread machine tin.

2. Scatter the flour over the mixture.

3. Add salt, milk powder and butter in different areas inside of tin.

4. Create a small hole in the middle of the mixture, place inside it the yeast.

5. Set the machine for basic-normal setting, medium crust and begin bread making process.

6. Add the sultanas when the machine is beeping or after the first kneading. When the bread is finished, remove it from the tin and place it on a wire rack to cool.

29. Light Rye and Caraway Bread

Rye flour adds a slightly sour flavour to the bread. Rye bread can be dense, so the flour is usually mixed with wheat flour to lighten the texture of the bread.

Servings: 2-4
Preparation time: 60-80 minutes

Ingredients:

- 1 cup of rye flour
- 1 ½ tablespoons of sunflower oil
- 2 tablespoons of lemon juice
- 1 ½ cups of water
- 3 ½ cups f white bread flour
- 1 ½ tablespoons of skimmed milk powder
- 1 teaspoon of dried yeast
- 1 tablespoon of light muscovado sugar
- 1 ½ teaspoons of salt
- 1 ½ teaspoons of caraway seeds

Directions:

1. Place the water, lemon juice, and sunflower oil into the bread machine tin.

2. Scatter the white and rye flour over the mixture.

3. Scatter the caraway seeds and skimmed milk too.

4. Add salt and sugar in different areas within the tin.

5. Create a small hole in the middle of the mixture and place inside it the yeast.

6. Set the machine to the basic-normal setting, medium crust and begin the bread making process.

7. When the bread is done, remove it from the tin and place it on a wire rack to cool.

30. Grainy Beer & Mustard Loaf

When serving the traditional ploughman's, lunch serve some chunks of this bread with some cheese and pickle. Try to use some pale ale for a subtler taste or brown ale for a stronger flavour of the bread. Open the beer at least 1 hour before using in the recipe to make sure it will be flat.

Servings: 2-4
Preparation time: 60-80 minutes

Ingredients:

- 1 tablespoon of vegetable oil
- 1 teaspoon of dried yeast
- 2 teaspoons of granulated sugar
- 1 ½ teaspoons of salt
- 1 ½ tablespoons of skimmed milk powder
- 1 1/3 cups of whole-meal flour
- 3 cups of white bread flour
- 3 tablespoons of wholegrain mustard
- 1 ¼ cups of flat beer

Directions:

1. Place the beer and vegetable oil inside of the bread machine tin.

2. Add the wholegrain mustard to tin.

3. Scatter the white, whole-meal flour on top of the mixture.

4. Scatter in the skimmed milk powder too.

5. Add the salt and sugar in different areas in the tin.

6. Create a small hole in the middle of the mixture, and add to it the yeast.

7. Set the machine to the basic-normal setting, medium crust and begin the bread making process.

8. When the bread is done, remove it from the tin and place it on a wire rack to cool.

Conclusion

We would like to personally acknowledge all our readers for downloading this book and giving their precious time to learn to prepare delicious bread at home. This book unveils an easy and pleasant way of preparing bread to enjoy it for your breakfast, meals and as desserts.

The book aims at providing the most comprehensive collection of bread recipes that our readers can easily prepare in their oven with minimal equipment and great taste.

Thank you again. Happy Bread Making!

www.ingramcontent.com/pod-product-compliance
Lightning Source LLC
LaVergne TN
LVHW012337290125
802515LV00008B/367